I'm a Part
of
God's Plan

by Frankie Falkner

Published by Woman's Missionary Union®
P.O. Box 830010
Birmingham, AL 35283-0010

©2002 by Woman's Missionary Union®
Printed in China
Woman's Missionary Union® and WMU® are registered trademarks.

Dewey Decimal Classification: CE
Subject Headings: God (Christianity) — Children's Literature
Christian Life — Children

ISBN: 1-56309-603-X
W028107 • 0602 • 5M (First printing)

To my parents who faithfully encouraged me to follow God's plan for my life.

God has a plan for everything.
God has a plan for me, too.

I'm glad I'm a
part of God's plan.

God planned for flowers to grow.

I'm a part of God's plan because He planned for me to grow too. I know I am growing when I have to get new shoes or when I am taller than my little sister.

God planned for the sun to shine during the day and the moon to shine at night.

I'm a part of God's plan because He planned for me to play during the day and sleep at night. When the sun comes up, I like to go outside and enjoy the day. It feels good to run and play in the sunshine. When the moon comes up, I say my prayers and go fast asleep.

God planned for the world to have many colors.

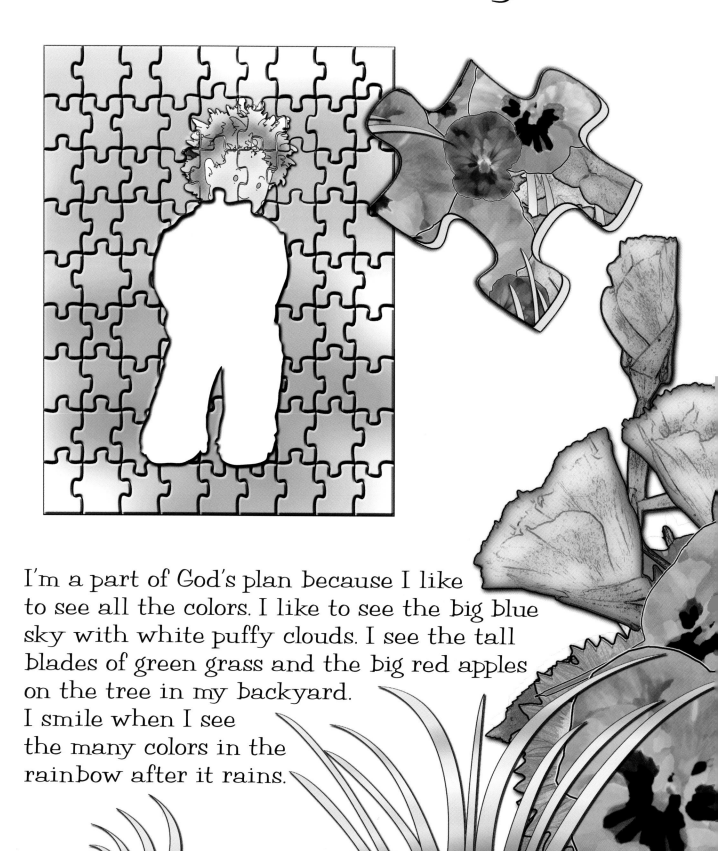

I'm a part of God's plan because I like
to see all the colors. I like to see the big blue
sky with white puffy clouds. I see the tall
blades of green grass and the big red apples
on the tree in my backyard.
I smile when I see
the many colors in the
rainbow after it rains.

God planned for kittens to be soft and for rocks to be hard.

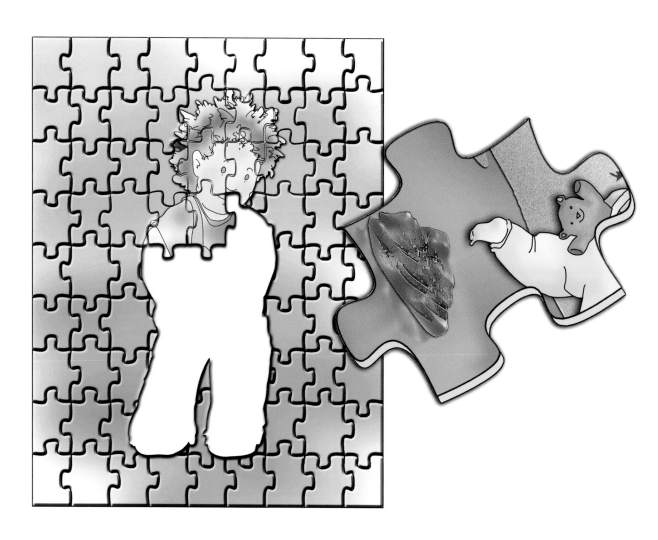

I'm a part of God's plan because I can touch my soft furry kitten and my fuzzy yellow bear. I can feel the rough rocks on the bottom of my feet as I tiptoe to the creek.

God planned for people to have good food to eat.

I'm a part of God's plan because I like to eat crispy fresh vegetables and juicy ripe fruit. I like to go to the store and help my mom find my favorite fruit. Sometimes I pack a peach or an orange, or some grapes with my lunch.

Mmmmmmmmm.......

God planned for different kinds of families.

I'm a part of God's plan because I have a family. My family likes to go to church. Sometimes we play outside or we read a good book together. My family loves each other. We work together.

God planned for each family member to help one another.

I'm a part of God's plan because
I help my family. I help my mother
pick up my toys. My dad likes it when
I help him rake the leaves. My grandmother
gives me a big smile when I make her cards and
sing my favorite songs to her.

God planned for people to have friends.

I'm a part of God's plan because I have friends. I like to play on the sliding board with my friends at the park.

We go Z O O O O O O O m

as we slide down. My friends and I like to play with the blocks at church. We build tall towers and laugh out loud when we knock them down to the ground!

God planned for people to be special.

I'm a part of God's plan because I am special. No one is just like me. You are special because there is no one just like you. God made each one of us special. How are you special?

God planned for people to read the Bible and learn about Jesus.

I'm a part of God's plan because I am learning about Jesus. I like hearing Bible stories about Jesus and all the great people in the Bible. The Bible is my favorite book. I turn the pages very carefully and I like to look at the pictures in my Bible.

God planned for people to love one another.

I'm a part of God's plan because I love others. I show love when I help someone who is hurt. I love others by sharing my toys. I tell my friends and my family that I love them very much.

God planned for people to talk to Him.

I'm a part of God's plan because I talk to Him. I talk to God and thank Him for my mommy and daddy. I thank Him for my friends and teachers, too. I like to thank God for good food before I eat my meals. I can thank God for my toys.

God planned for Jesus to come and show us how to treat others.

I'm a part of God's plan because I want to be like Jesus. I am like Jesus when I tell others how much God loves them. I am like Jesus when I read my Bible and pray. I am like Jesus when I am kind and help others.

Thank You, God, that You have a plan for me. I'm glad to know that I'm a part of God's plan.